THE COLD - WAR
MURDER

The Frame-up Against
Ethel and Julius.
ROSENBERG

By RICHARD O. BOYER

INTRODUCTION

By William L. Patterson

Ethel and Julius Rosenberg are today in the death house in Sing Sing prison, Ossining, New York. The prosecutor who conducted the trial is, so recent hearings of the New York Crime Commission reveal, an acquaintance of leading gangsters and racketeers. He has been promoted to a judgeship. The Federal judge who handed down the death sentence has decreed that it shall be carried out during the week of January 12, 1953. He too is seeking advancement, and refuses to intercede in reduction of this inexcusable sentence. The Supreme Court has twice refused to review the case, righteously asserting on each occasion that its refusal does not constitute an endorsement of the proceedings of the trial court. For the Rosenberg family, and for a justice-loving public, there can be only horror at this hollow gesture.

You, the people, thus become the Court of Last Appeal. This introduction is addressed to you.

If the President of the United States is to exercise the clemency with which he is endowed, your militant appeals will supply the motive power. The Rosenbergs from death cells cannot present the Chief Executive with the facts upon which they rest their plea for the right to live. That is your responsibility. It is a responsibility not only to this man and woman, who have not yet had their day in an unprejudiced court before a jury of their peers. It is a responsibility as well to all progressive humanity, which will judge our attitude toward this family as inexorably as it judged the German people, whose words "We knew not what they did" could not absolve them of complicity in the Nazi crimes.

Upon our failure to speak out, to act for the Rosenbergs, history may write the final chapter in their lives. But the record in the case will not be closed. The proof of its enduring character is pregnant in the facts we here present. Failure to act becomes complicity in an awful crime.

The death of Ethel and Julius Rosenberg will resolve

no problem with which you are concerned, no problem of defense, yet the interest of the people in the gravest domestic issue with which we are confronted—that of safeguarding our Constitutional liberties against the drive of those who would black out free speech and other civil rights—will be seriously weakened if they die. Their lives have already merged, in the eyes of thinking people throughout the world, with the question of the quality of American justice and democracy. We might well carry this momentous idea further: today there is no issue of democracy that is not interwoven with the issue of peace. Through this relationship we link the lives of these two people with the danger of war.

You may not see the Rosenberg case as part of that great world drama. If you fix your responsibility to them in a narrower circle, it is not diminished. So long as they live, that responsibility will not die, for you cannot accept this punishment so far excessive of the alleged crime. Your responsibility is limited only by your love of justice, your moral strength, your acceptance of the American people's sense of fair play. Let your role be determined by the knowledge that the people could have saved Sacco and Vanzetti.

You can act singly. We can act together. Address yourself to the president with a plea for clemency. Head a delegation of your neighbors to Washington to request executive clemency. Take part in every demonstration that raises the cry: "The Rosenbergs shall not die!" Carry that cry everywhere you go. Prepare to join the picket line before the White House in December. Let no distorted sense of what is proper decorum deter you. Everything is proper that will save them.

The lives of Ethel and Julius Rosenberg can be saved. They can be set free. The Supreme Court by decree has placed the final appeal in your hands. Prepare yourself to act untiringly, fearlessly.

There are those who advise calm and restraint. The conscience of America will be awakened only by an angry people. Legal murder calls for righteous indignation and militant action. The dead cannot be brought back. Those about to be orphaned, those about to die, command you!

THE COLD-WAR
MURDER

By RICHARD O. BOYER

I. "LIKE OTHERS WE SPOKE FOR PEACE"

"I will be as harsh as truth and as uncompromising as justice. On this subject I do not wish to think, or speak, or write with moderation. I will not equivocate, I will not excuse, I will not retreat a single inch, and I will be heard! The apathy of the people is enough to make every statue leap from its pedestal, and to hasten the resurrection of the dead."

> William Lloyd Garrison, in the first issue of *The Liberator*, January 1, 1831.

WHEN THE NEWS CAME they received it quietly enough. After all, there had been no peak of hope or depth of despair that this ordinary man and wife, guilty of nothing save fighting for peace and the Bill of Rights, had not suffered during their 660 days and nights in Sing Sing's death house. The nights were the worst, for it was then that they could not protect themselves from the thoughts of their two small boys. This was just one thing more—one other time when they could not break, but could only know that decent people would still somehow save them from death, from the monstrous fabrication that they had stolen the secret of the atom bomb.

The principal keeper, or the PK as he is known in the precincts of Sing Sing, told them on the morning of November 22, 1952. He stopped first before the cell of Julius Rosenberg, ruddy-cheeked and vital, a large and handsome young man, who was playing chess, calling out his moves to the unseen occupant of another death-house cell. He was wearing a white shirt and gray denim trousers of prison issue. He had not shaved yet and his mustache was bristly.

The PK told him, quickly, that he and his wife, Ethel, were to die during the week of January 12, 1953, unless they were saved by the executive clemency of President Truman. Fifty-one days. There was a look on Rosenberg's face that the keeper, or so he said later, did not enjoy, and he turned away quickly.

He was climbing a steel stairway toward the cell of Ethel Rosenberg, when he heard her singing. She once sang in a choir, and the scores of symphonies and operas have been a comfort to her in the women's section of the death house where she is alone, the only occupant. Later the matron told him that it was a Brahms lullaby, one that had been a favorite of her children. She must have heard his steps, for the song stopped abruptly. Her serious, sensitive face was framed by the bars of her cell when he stood before her. She did not move. She said no word. She was still standing there, her hands clenched to the bars, when he left.

The head keeper seemed a trifle upset when he told the Rosenbergs' lawyer about it. "She's so little," he said. "Why, she can't be more than five feet in height." Most of the prison guards like the Rosenbergs. They know they are not criminals. For that matter, virtually everyone who has studied the case knows that the Rosenbergs are sacrifices to the

Moloch that is the atom-bomb, that superweapon which became a fetish and came into being with a flash that killed 60,000 men, women, and children. It has been perfected, the press reports, until one bomb can now level a city and kill 600,000.

Almost everyone who has examined the trial record feels that the Rosenbergs are victims of the cult of the atom bomb: of the fantastic mania of "secrecy" about that which scientists say is already known; a pretended secrecy used to foment sentiment for war.

They believe that the young Jewish parents are human sacrifices to what Supreme Court Justice Douglas called "the black silence of fear," to the panic that ambitious politicians use to hide their graft and obtain their ends.

They point to the fact that the savage peacetime sentence against the Rosenbergs is absolutely unprecedented, the first of its kind in American history; that Axis Sally and Tokyo Rose, as well as at least four other Americans found guilty of treason during World War II, received sentences of ten years while Ilse Koch, the Nazi murderess of Buchenwald, has been set free by the American authorities in Germany. Dr. Klaus Fuchs, a confessed atom bomb spy, received a sentence of fourteen years in England, while Dr. Allan Nunn May, another confessed atomic spy, received a sentence half that long. They note that a member of the armed forces of the United States in Korea, recently charged with selling jet plane secrets to the North Koreans, faces a maximum sentence of life imprisonment.

Many of those who have interested themselves in the case, including leaders in the fields of religion, science, art, and labor, are disturbed by the fact that Federal Judge Irving R. Kaufman, who sentenced the Rosenbergs to death, declared in doing so that this ordinary man and wife from New York's East Side were responsible for the Korean War. He said they were guilty (although they had been neither charged with nor tried for such a crime) of contributing to

50,000 American casualties on battlefields they had never seen, eight thousand miles away.

Those who have concerned themselves with this case— and they extend across the nation, they circle the world, they are of every religious and political faith—believe that the two young parents are the victims of perjured testimony of those who, having confessed, did then, in order to save themselves from death, falsely incriminate others. There are millions who feel that the punishment meted out is far in excess of the crime this man and woman are alleged to have committed.

These are the reasons why a great national and international movement is increasing by the day and hour, thousands on thousands of people demanding that President Truman grant executive clemency to the Rosenbergs, that their effort to establish their innocence shall not be silenced forever in the electric chair.

Everywhere men and women are recalling the Sacco-Vanzetti case, recalling that their innocence was finally admitted, but only after their execution. Everywhere, as they work, they resolve that it must not happen again. Innocence established after death will not return the parents of orphaned children.

In Chicago and New York, in Los Angeles and Detroit, Catholic priests, Protestant ministers, and Jewish rabbis; trade union officials who remember Tom Mooney and know that the Rosenbergs have been active trade unionists; Negro leaders who know the anatomy of frame-up better than any other Americans, are combining to save this country from a precedent that has no logic unless it is to silence those who voice unpopular views.

In Paris, poet Paul Eluard, hero of the underground, on his deathbed penned an appeal for the Rosenbergs. He had seen such killings under the Nazis, he wrote, but had believed them impossible under a democracy. In Paris, too, as they picket the American Embassy, they speak of the

8

Dreyfus case, for there are in the Rosenbergs' trial, as this pamphlet will further show, overtones of the anti-Semitic that will not down.

In Great Britain, scores of the country's leading scientists, some of its leading barristers, hundreds of university professors, actors, and artists, as well as the London Trades Union Council, representing 600,000 English trade union members, demand that the Rosenbergs shall not die.

In Jerusalem, twenty of Israel's religious leaders cable President Truman: "We are not aware of any precedent where a person has been condemned to death in a democratic country for offenses alleged, as in this case, in time of peace." From Cleveland and San Francisco, from Boston and Alabama, Tokyo and Iowa, Bombay and Indiana, men and women of good will are writing President Truman asking for clemency. For this is a case, like the Dreyfus case, that stirs the conscience of mankind.

What problems will the death of the Rosenbergs solve for the American people?

The hour is late and the forces of reaction strong; but if you read this pamphlet, and pursue the detailed proof of that which has been stated here, you will see, I think, why a victory must be won. As for the Rosenbergs, they have two beliefs. The first is in their innocence. The second is in their fellow-citizens.

II. "YOU WHO ARE FREE TODAY . . ."

> "We are not martyrs or heroes, nor do we wish to be. But we will not pay the price that is asked of us, to betray our hopes for the peaceful, neighborly, democratic world which our children and all children need if they are to carry on the human race.
>
> "We do not pretend that we are unafraid. But we fear also for those for whom our death sentence is a precedent, for those who like us may find themselves in our place, unless you, who are free today, make us free again."
>
> Julius and Ethel Rosenberg writing from Sing Sing's death house.

THE ROSENBERGS' ARREST came almost as unexpectedly as a bolt of lightning from a cloudless sky. Before they could get their bearings, almost before they knew with what they were charged, they were jerked from the quiet of their home, their children thrust into an institution, flashlights burst in their faces as photographers clamored, they were interrogated constantly by the F.B.I., they were immediately jailed and held in bail so high they could not raise it, and every engine of public opinion, above all the press and the radio, was day upon day thundering the word "Guilty!"

Not the least incredible part of it was that the chief witness against them was Ethel Rosenberg's own brother, David Greenglass, the enemy of her husband. He confessed himself an atomic spy. Did he purchase his own life and that of his wife, who also confessed, by dooming his sister and her husband?

And then there was the unbelievable trial. Every good thing they had ever done, such as their fight against Spanish fascism, was introduced as evidence of their guilt. There was the unprecedented charge of the trial judge that they were guilty of starting a war half a world away. And then they found themselves in Sing Sing's death house.

From the first, Julius and Ethel Rosenberg knew that they must draw upon the last reserves of their great courage if they were not to break. Their innocence meant little when their frail human bodies, their simple average personalities, were pitted against all the vast impersonal power of a government seemingly intent on killing them. They took for their motto, repeating it constantly in their letters: "Courage, Confidence, Perspective." They thought of themselves as representatives of the American people, of ordinary people everywhere, fighting against tyranny, against world war and a growing fascism. If they could repel the moments of terror and horror that were sometimes theirs, if they could fight on, the people they represented would too, for they and the people were one. And their courage made them proud, and, sometimes, almost happy.

From the first, too, it had been possible, and it remained possible, for them to save themselves from death if they would "confess" and implicate the leaders of a political party which was everywhere being castigated. They could live if they would live a lie. Only a few words, and they would live. But, as they said, "We will not pay the price that is asked of us, to betray our hopes for the peaceful, neighborly, democratic world which our children and all

11

children need if they are to carry on the human race." They chose death, if that must be, rather than betray the American people, rather than become a party to fixing death as a penalty for dissent from war.

> *"Only a word, only a lie,*
> *To change your destiny.*
> *Recall, reflect, remember long*
> *How sweet the mornings be."**

The Rosenbergs were sentenced to death—the formal charge was conspiracy to commit espionage—on April 5, 1951. By April 15, Ethel Rosenberg was in Sing Sing's death house while her husband remained in the federal detention house in New York City. On April 17, she wrote him:

"My own very dearest husband: I have already embarked on the next lap of our history-making journey. The bars of my large, comfortable cell hold several books; the lovely, colorful cards (including your exquisite birthday greeting to me) that I accumulated at the House of Detention, line the top ledge of my writing table to pleasure the eyes and brighten the spirit.

"The children's snapshots are taped onto a 'picture frame' made of cardboard, and smile sweetly at me whenever I so desire, and somewhere within me I shall find that 'courage, confidence, and perspective' I shall need to see me through the days and nights of bottomless horror, of tortured screams I may not utter, of frenzied longing I must deny!

"Bunny, I'll have to write you a second letter

---

* From The Ballad of One Who Sang at the Stake, by Louis Aragon. This was a poem written in memory of Gabriel Peri, editor of L'Humanite, executed by the Nazis during their occupation of Paris.

after this one goes out as I don't want to keep you waiting a minute longer for word from me."

To which her husband replied:

"Dearest Ethel: I received your wonderful letter this afternoon. The first impression I got is that the situation as it confronted you was overwhelming and to some degree you were emotionally shocked. If our lawyers do not succeed in bringing you back to the Women's Detention House I will move heaven and earth to be sent to Sing Sing to be nearer you and to be able to see you whenever it is possible.

"It is impossible to keep the truth and facts of our case hidden from the public. Sooner or later the true picture, the real facts, will become known to all. Many people have already expressed to our lawyers and my family, their sentiments and desire to help us. Take heart and know that we are not alone, and that the monstrous sentence passed on us which at first stunned the people, will, as time goes on, result in an avalanche of protest and this great movement, coupled to our legal fight, will set us free.

"Sweetheart, I am not trying to minimize all the difficulties you face. Believe me, I am fully aware of all the nightmares, the pain and hurt you feel. My heart cries out for you and I want so to shield and protect you and be with you in this time of need and to hold in my arms. Yet I feel so sure of you that I just know you will always be there and that is the assurance that we will some day find each other again and go back, as you say, to our precious life and wonderful family."

In mid-May, 1951, Julius Rosenberg was successful in his efforts to be transferred to Sing Sing's death house that he might be near his wife. They met for the first time in

13

six weeks. Then Ethel Rosenberg wrote her husband:

"Can we ever forget the turbulence and struggle, the joy and beauty of the early years of our relationship when you courted me and I accepted you as my heart's dearest? Together we hunted down the answers to all the seemingly insoluble riddles a complex and callous society presented.

"For the sake of those answers, for the sake of American democracy, justice, and brotherhood, for the sake of peace and bread and roses, and the innocent laughter of little children, we shall continue to sit here in dignity and pride and in the deep and abiding knowledge of our innocence before God and man until the truth becomes a clarion call to all decent humanity and the doors of this slaughter house are flung wide!

"There was once a wise man, I forget his name, who marveled at the 'indestructibility of human character.' Beloved, we shall prove him right; perhaps then will other human beings believe in their indestructibility, too, and rally in ever-increasing numbers to our defense and their own. For they who have the courage and the foresight and the decency to aid the Rosenbergs' fight for freedom, ensure their own eventual release."

Such moments of exaltation do not come every day to Ethel Rosenberg. She has to fight for them. Sometimes she tries to sink into the dull routine of prison life, to clutch at normalcy through it. "My darling sweethearts," she wrote to her two small boys, Michael, eight, and Robert, five, on November 8, 1951, "I have just had a shower and dinner. I am writing at my desk and listening to the radio. The Longines 'Symphonette' is playing Brahms' Lullaby and I am remembering how I used to sing you both to sleep at home. You see, pussy cats, tough as it is to be separated from you,

14

and much as we miss one another, there can never be any forgetting when there has been the kind of love we have had—Daddy and Mike and Robbie and Mommy—all four of us together!"

As the days and weeks went on, it seemed increasingly strange that almost her only contact with her husband, some hundred feet away but in another tier of the death house cells, was through the United States mails. Each day she would write, "Julius Rosenberg, 354 Hunter Street, Ossining, N. Y.," knowing that at the same instant her husband, almost within reach, was writing, "Mrs. Ethel Rosenberg, 354 Hunter Street, Ossining, N. Y." 354 Hunter Street! What a discreet designation for a death house!

They see each other for an hour once a week when a cage on wheels is placed before her cell. It is divided by a heavy wire screen and has a door at each end. She enters one end from her cell and sits before the wire mesh. He enters the other end. It is difficult for them to see each other but they can at least speak and hear and be near.

For some reason the time she hates the worst is the exercise hour each afternoon at four. The "exercise yard" is a cement cubicle, twenty feet by eighteen, formed by high walls. There is no top and she can see the sky. Sometimes the birds fly in and the death house matron has let her have bread to feed them. Once she saw an airplane and sometimes she hears the muted roar of a train. The beautiful Hudson River is just to the west of her but she cannot see it.

After such an hour she wrote her husband not long ago:

"A wintry sky and a sharp wind that carried gusts of rain sent me briskly stamping about the yard, as though by doing so I might stamp out the rising panic, the threatened assault upon my decent human courage. Darling, the unyielding loneliness which engages me in grim and continuous battle, took possession unopposed today; it sank its fangs

15

so deep that I wept helplessly. And yet my will persisted and refused to acknowledge defeat! Only the question beat dully within me. How much agony could the human heart contain without bursting?"

But on the same day she wrote her children:

"My Darling Sweethearts: It is evening and I am listening to the radio and trying to imagine what my honey bunnies might be doing. It was so cold and windy outdoors today that I was not able to play handball. So I watched the birds eating the bread that I had scattered for them. They would hop, hop, hop after a little piece that the wind had blown right out of their mouths in such a comical way. The other day the sky was full of graceful little swallows and sometimes great sea gulls, all soft and gray and white, float lazily overhead."

About once every five weeks the Rosenbergs see their children. They are brought to the death house by Emanuel H. Bloch, their attorney. For days and weeks before the event the Rosenbergs write back and forth about it, planning each minute of the approaching visit, deciding the order in which each parent will talk to each child and for how long, and how many minutes will be devoted to each of the children's problems of which they have learned from letters. There is only one hour to accomplish so much. "Be sure," Julius wrote his wife before one visit, "to comfort our big fellow about his troubles with his handwriting."

They meet in the conference room at the death house and the main object of the parents is to cheer their children and reassure them. Julius tells them jokes and sometimes sees the fright disappear from their eyes and hears them laugh. The family has always liked music and sometimes they sing together. Ethel Rosenberg has never wept once when the boys were there.

III. BACKGROUND FOR MURDER

THE ROOTS OF POLITICAL MURDER, of "legal assassination," go deep and often have their being not in what any culprit has done, nor in any individual guilt, but in the needs of high policy. If people are to be mobilized for a dreadful war, history has shown again and again, proponents of peace may find themselves charged with strange, heinous crimes that smack of treason. If the status quo is yielding gargantuan profits, riches almost beyond accounting, critics of the status quo may be in danger as Christ found, and Elijah Lovejoy, and Harry T. Moore.

Prosecutors may secure political advancement, as they send peace advocates to death; judges may be promoted; officials may conceal their graft as they hound proponents of peace—but these are by-products of a much larger policy. The victims are sometimes almost incidental—what is important is the policy of war and mobilizing for war, the policy of racial and religious hatred and intimidation. Nonetheless there must be victims, and although they are often unknown unfortunates caught in a vast struggle that covers continents and seas and includes peoples and armies and chancelleries and billions on billions of dollars, still these victims of high policy have always moved the human heart.

Even when the single murder for policy's sake grows into genocide, as when six million Jews were slain by the Nazis as a part of their subjugating the entire German people under fascism, we cannot, must not forget the single, private, naked person out of whose torture policy was made,

17

and profits were made; out of whose agony other people were frightened into acquiescence.

And while the identity of those murdered is only incidental to *haute politique,* to the vast end to which their deaths are intended to contribute, if only a little, still it is necessary to select the victims with some care. It helps the politicians. for example, if the victims are active trade unionists. It helps still more if they are Jews. If they can be shown to have fought actively for the rights of the Negro people, they are almost automatically suspect. And if it can be charged that they are Communists—then it is just perfect. Never mind about the evidence, don't worry about the facts, perjury is justified when serving this high and patriotic end and a conviction is as certain as approving editorials.

In speaking of background, therefore, let us begin at the beginning with the lives of Julius and Ethel Rosenberg and find out why they were eligible for murder—high level policy murder, cold-war murder.

Julius Rosenberg was born on New York's lower East Side, the youngest of four children, two boys and two girls, in 1918, the last year of the First World War. Like millions of others living there he came of a religious and working-class background, of a family in which music and learning were honored. Ethel, born three years earlier and not far away, attended the same public schools that Julius attended. Julius' father, dead now, was a union man, a member of the Amalgamated Clothing Workers. Strikes were frequent in what was then a sweatshop industry. The family remembers long lean days when their only comfort was the synagogue. The elder Rosenberg was finally blacklisted for his efforts to build the union. Times were increasingly hard until the children were old enough to produce some income.

In a letter stamped approved by Censor 5, Julius wrote:

"My parents were orthodox religious people, and we children avidly learned the history and culture

18

and traditions of our forefathers. I was able to receive a Hebrew education that included a couple of years at the High School level. When I graduated with honors from the Down Town Talmud Torah I made a twelve page speech in Hebrew and just about that time I was vice-president of the Young Men's Synagogue Organization.

"The free public schools of the East Side taught the fine democratic traditions of our country inherited from the founding fathers. Community activities ingrained fair play as a cardinal principle of our lives. With such a fruitful heritage as my foundation, and being socially conscious, it was only natural that I always worked to improve existing conditions for the common people, for a better, happier world.

"In the natural course of events I became known among our people on the East Side as a liberal and progressive thinker."

Julius was a serious boy given to long, long thoughts about the state of the world. It hurt him deeply when he found that much of the Constitution was a mockery as far as the fifteen million American Negroes were concerned, and he resolved to fight for its extension to them.

Julius was fourteen when Hitler came to power, using among other things the big lie that Jews everywhere and always were traitors and should be exterminated, as a part of Nazi preparation for world war. An important factor in Hitler's drive for power and war was the huge frame-up that was the Reichstag fire trial. There were millions upon millions then who believed that this trial, fabricated completely by the Nazis, was a true trial for a real crime—but now there is not a responsible person in the world who does not know that it was a frame-up. A frame-up, consisting of manufactured evidence and perfectly tailored testimony, cut

19

to meet the needs of the prosecution is the hardest kind of case in the world for the innocent to win.

But with the election of Roosevelt in 1932, and with the New Deal backed by millions, Julius Rosenberg began to learn something of the power of the people.

He was seventeen when he entered City College in 1935 and already stories were coming out of Germany of the murders of his people in Buchenwald and Dachau. The next year he met Ethel Greenglass, a tiny and sensitive girl who wrote poetry, sang in the Schola Cantorum as its youngest member, studied music at Carnegie Hall, and was a player in the Clark House Dramatic Group. She was earning her living then as a typist and lived on Sheriff Street on Manhattan's East Side. She had a lovely voice, certain and true and tender, and Julius particularly liked to hear her sing the lieder of Brahms and Schubert and Schumann. Often they talked late into the night; sometimes they walked the streets beneath the towers of Gotham, glimpsing the moon as it slipped by between the buildings, and always talking, talking endlessly, talking of how peace could be made eternal, and people happy and prosperous, and how then there would be laughter and fountains and sunlight instead of the groans and torture of concentration camps.

They thrilled to the Spanish people's defense of Madrid, spoke up for collective security to prevent World War II and throttle fascism, defended President Roosevelt's speech which called for "quarantining the aggressor," suffered as Kaltenborn described over the radio Chamberlain's sell-out to Hitler at Munich in 1938. They spoke of poetry and philosophy, too, and they were very much in love and very much in earnest when they said that they would give all of their lives and all of their strength that their children, and children everywhere, should know nothing of racist persecution and war.

Julius was graduated in 1939 with a degree in electrical engineering and a few months later he and Ethel were mar-

20

ried. They had no money, of course, but they had been children of the depression and they were used to doubling up and making out. They moved in with Julius' mother. In 1940 Ethel got a job in Washington as a typist in the Census Bureau. They hated the separation but Julius could get nothing but odd jobs; he did some research work for an inventor and some tool designing for a Brooklyn firm. Contracts for war had yet to finally rout the depression. The war came in 1939, and they suffered when the Nazis overran Poland, and then France, and then all of Europe while the Jewish people were slain by the millions.

Julius wanted to help defeat Hitler. He was certain that the United States would be attacked by the Axis, certain that humanity could not advance until fascism was defeated. He applied for and obtained a position as a civilian employee, a junior engineer in the Army Signal Corps at $2,000 a year. The job was in New York and Ethel returned from Washington. The couple borrowed some furniture from friends (this is relevant in that it was later charged that they lived in affluence on Russian gold) .and succeeded in getting a three-room apartment, rent $45.75 a month, in the housing development on New York's East Side known as Knickerbocker Village. They lived there for almost ten years.

Julius worked ardently for the Signal Corps, supervising private firms in the production of electronic communication, radio telephones and other field equipment. Then came December 7, and Pearl Harbor. Ethel was now working as hard as he was, as a volunteer in civilian defense.

Julius was filled with a great hope that the Allies would be victorious when the Nazis suffered their first great defeat at Stalingrad, in 1943. His eldest son, Michael, was born in 1944 and the two young parents worked even harder, determined that their son should have a better fate than death in war or a concentration camp. In common with many other patriots then, Julius had been insistently demanding a second

21

front in Western Europe. President Roosevelt was demanding it, too, and so was General Eisenhower, but this point counted heavily against the young engineer some years later when insistence on a second front was considered evidence of treason. Nor did the Rosenbergs forget the people of Spain, suffering under Franco. Collecting money for Spanish refugee children, they stood on street corners, rattling coin-filled cans as they asked for contributions. This, too, was later to be considered one of the damning pieces of evidence against them.

A symbol of the new era was the dropping of the world's first atomic bomb in August of 1945, killing some 60,000 men, women, and children at Hiroshima.

By the time the bomb was dropped, Ethel's youngest brother, David Greenglass, a mechanic, had been in the army for more than two years, stationed since 1944, the Rosenbergs were told, near Albuquerque, New Mexico. When he was home on furlough late in 1944 and early in 1945, the Rosenbergs frequently saw him, and his wife, Ruth, at family gatherings. David, a plump young man who suffered from what his doctor called "psychological heart disease," was full of plans for making money after the war. He had always seemed a little amused by Julius' idealism, particularly by his heated arguments for a second front.

Yet the Greenglasses looked up to Julius. He was a college graduate and he knew what he believed in. On a furlough in January, 1945, David told his family, including his sister and brother-in-law, that he was working on a secret project at Los Alamos, New Mexico and his relatives admired and respected his part in the war, solemnly refraining from asking anything about it. Still the Rosenbergs were worried when Ruth Greenglass later told Julius that she was frightened because Dave had made some remark about stealing something at Los Alamos "and making some money." Julius said later that he thought it must concern machine parts or gasoline for black market speculation for

22

there were a good many stories in the newspapers then about such things.

"Listen," he said with all the authority of an elder brother admonishing reckless kids, "tell Dave to lay off that kind of stuff. He'll only get in a jam."

Before the war ended, and with the country's political climate already beginning to change, Julius was fired by the Signal Corps. His talk about a second front and the Russian all-out war effort had apparently been reported to his superiors. He was charged with being a Communist. In addition, he had been exceedingly active as chairman of the grievance committee for federal employees in his union, the Federation of Architects and Engineers. He tried to fight the dismissal, went to see his Congressman in Washington about it, but before he could do anything more the war was over.

David was back, out of the Army and eager to get to work and make some money. Julius, David, and Bernard Greenglass, another brother of Ethel's as well as a fourth investor not in the family and not active in the business, formed a partnership in 1946. They opened a machine shop at 370 Houston Street. From the first, business went badly; and from the first David was resentful at the fact that it seemed increasingly likely that he would lose the money, probably about $1,500, that he had borrowed and put into the business. They were all worried. Quarrels became frequent and bitter.

Julius might have been discouraged were it not for his family. But when he went home at night and entered his own little cubicle in the vast housing project, almost a town in itself, he closed the door on a troubled world. They had built something together, he and Ethel, in these three small rooms, their windows shining in the darkness, that pitted fragile human happiness, with little more weight and substance than laughter or a baby's voice, against the huge forces threatening the welfare of mankind. Robert was born in

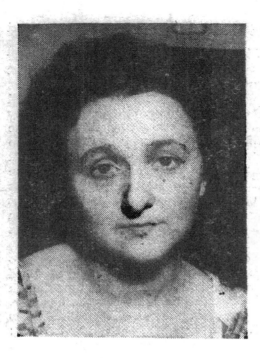

**E HEL
ROSENBERG**

1947. The Rosenbergs bought a second-hand upright for $25 and they had pleasant evenings singing and playing with the children.

Still, there were times after Julius had gone to bed on winter nights, lying awake and hearing the wind whistle around the buildings, and the mournful moan of a tugboat on the East River, when he could not help thinking of the direction of events.

Anti-Semitism increased. Spy scares and hysteria pyramided to unprecedented heights. There were loyalty pledges,

24

**JULIUS
ROSENBERG**

in which people gained a precarious safety by signing state-
ments. Teachers were being fired, writers jailed, actors boy-
cotted. There was no quicker way to be marked as a
Communist than to advocate world peace, unless it was to
defend the Bill of Rights. Informers were honored by public
proclamation—there was a Philbrick Day in Boston and a
Cvetic Day in Pittsburgh—and newspapers, radio, and mo-
tion pictures contained little more than accounts of probable
war and Red penetration.

It was said that the State Department was dominated

25

by Communists, and the loyalty of even the Secretary of State was questioned, even that of General Marshall.

W. E. B. DuBois, world-famous scholar and elder statesman of the Negro people, was actually indicted for advocating world peace, charged with being a foreign agent.

There were hundreds of arrests, scores of legislative investigations, attacks against the foreign-born, against the Negro people, trial after trial, and for the first time in the nation's history Americans were being imprisoned for their political views in trials under the Smith Act in which books, known and read the world over, were the main evidence.

Julius might have read, and probably did, Cyrus Sulzberger's story in the *New York Times* of May 21, 1946, declaring that the hysteria had been deliberately created. "... The momentum of pro-Soviet feeling," Sulzberger had written, "had continued too heavily after the armistice. Th... made it difficult for the Administration to carry out the stiffer diplomatic policy required now. For this reason a campaign was worked up." Later the *U. S. News and World Report* declared (February 17, 1951): "War scares are easy to create." And the American Civil Liberties Union in reviewing the year 1947 declared: "Excitement bordering on hysteria characterized the public approach to any issue related to Communism." With wages frozen, and profits higher than ever in history, four and a half times larger than the peak year of 1929, averaging 48 billions a year before taxes after the Korean "police action," there were talks of "peace scares" and their adverse effect on the stock market and an economy based on war. The *U. S. News and World Report* warned its readers in 1950 that "Peace moves by Russia right now would embarrass the U. S. If a real 'peace scare' should now develop ... the boom would crack."

Perhaps Julius sometimes worried about his forthright stand for world peace and the Bill of Rights. It would be dangerous for a man in business to find himself labeled a Communist in the present climate. But he thought it his duty

26

as an American to warn of policies he felt would bring disaster and death to the American people. He had other things to worry about, too. David Greenglass was becoming increasingly jumpy. He was nervous and moody and sometimes Julius thought that his brother-in-law was on the verge of a breakdown. In February of 1950 David mumbled something about the F. B. I. paying a visit to his house, but he seemed to be sorry he had mentioned it and added nothing more. His condition made it no easier for Julius to carry out his plan of buying out his partners. Julius thought that $600 would be about right for his payment to David since he had loaned Dave money. But David felt that $1,500 was nearer the correct figure.

In the middle of May, 1950, David appeared at the machine shop at Houston Street. Julius told about it later at the trial when he testified:

> Well, about the middle of May, I can't tell the exact date, David came to my shop one morning. He came into my office. I was sitting in my office and he said, "Come on outside, I want to talk to you."
>
> I said, "Look Dave, I got to conduct my business. Let us talk here."
>
> He said, "No, it is important. Let us go outside." We walked to the Hamilton Fish Park, right opposite my shop on Houston Street. Dave said to me, "Julie, you got to get me $2,000. I need it at once."
>
> I said, "Look Dave, you know the arrangements I made with you. I am obligated to Dave Schein. (Another partner.) I gave him a down payment of $1,000. I have no cash left. You can't get blood out of a stone. I just don't have the money. What do you want it for?"
>
> He said, "I need the money. Don't ask me questions."

27

I said, "Dave, you are getting very excited. What's the matter with you?"

So he said, "Well if you can't help me like that maybe you can do something else for me. Will you get your doctor and ask him if he would make out a certificate for smallpox vaccination?" I said, "Why don't you go to your doctor?" and he said, "Don't ask me that. I can't do it."

And I said, "It is highly irregular but I will ask my doctor if he will do that." And he said, "Don't tell him who it is for and, incidentally, while you are talking to him ask if he knows what kind of injections are required to go to Mexico."

Julius was upset by this encounter. He went home and saw Ethel. "Your brother is in some kind of trouble," he said. "He's acting peculiar and I don't know what to do about it. I don't see why I'm the person to help him. You know he's had it in for me and our relations haven't been of the best." But Ethel said, "If Dave's in trouble, we have to help him. He's my kid brother." So a few days later Julius went to David's house and they walked to the East River Drive. The testimony of Julius resumes:

Dave was very excited. He was pale and he had a haggard look on his face. I said, "Calm yourself, take it easy. What's troubling you?" and he said, "Julie, I'm in a terrible jam. I can't tell you anything about it. All I want you to do for me, Julie, is I must have a couple of thousand dollars in cash."

I says, "David, I don't have the money on me, I can't raise that kind of money."

He says, "Julie, can't you borrow it from your relatives?"

I says, "Dave, I cannot do that."

He says, "Can you take it from the business?"

I says, "Dave, I cannot do that."

28

"Well, Julie," he said, "I just got to have that money. If you don't get me that money you are going to be sorry."

I said, "Look here, Dave, what are you trying to do? Threaten or blackmail me?"

Well, he was very excitable at this time, he was puffing and I saw a wild look in his eyes. I realized it was time to cut this conversation short. We had been walking down the Drive, near Houston or Stanton Street, and I said, "Look, Dave, you go home, take a cold shower, I have some work to do, I am going to the shop; good-bye."

David Greenglass was arrested on June 15. There were reports in the newspapers that he had confessed to being part of a conspiracy to commit espionage, that he had confessed to being paid for stealing the secret of the atom bomb while he was a soldier at Los Alamos. He had implicated his own wife, the newspapers said, and the penalty was death. Ruth Greenglass had just had a baby.

The F. B. I. held David Greenglass without bail and questioned him repeatedly. What would he do? If he gave the F. B. I. what they wanted—a basis for charging an alleged Communist with participating in atom bomb espionage for the benefit of the Soviet Union—his and his wife's lives would be saved. If he failed to "cooperate," the death penalty for both himself and his wife was a distinct possibility.

The answer as to what he would do was given 31 days later with the indictment of Julius Rosenberg, and it was spelled out more clearly through the testimony of David Greenglass at the trial. A month after her husband was taken from her, Ethel Rosenberg was taken from her children and placed in a cell.

IV. THE TRIAL

"The duty of securing a review rests on public opinion throughout the world."

D. N. Pritt, Queen's Counsel, former Member of the British Parliament.

THREE DIFFERENT INDICTMENTS were returned in succession, as David Greenglass continued to produce new ramifications to his story. The final indictment, returned January 31, 1951, named seven members of an alleged conspiracy to commit espionage in time of war in behalf of a foreign government, the Soviet Union.

Ruth Greenglass was not even indicted, although she had confessed to stealing atomic secrets and was named as one of the conspirators, nor was she arrested.

Her husband, David, was named as a defendant, but he was not tried. Instead, he was allowed to plead guilty after the Rosenberg trial, when he received a sentence of fifteen years, admitting that he hoped his testimony against the Rosenbergs would save him from the possibility of a death sentence.

Harry Gold was also named as a conspirator, but not as a defendant. He was already in prison, completely in the power of the government, under a thirty year sentence for confessed atomic espionage for money. It was manifest that he stood to gain if he pleased the prosecution by his testimony.

Max Elitcher, a friend of Julius, faced possible perjury charges in connection with another case. Elitcher also testified against the Rosenbergs; he said he was "scared to death," admitting that the government had power to send him to prison for perjury. Most of his testimony involved the third defendant, Morton Sobell, who received a sentence of thirty years.

Nevertheless, there was virtually no testimony against the Rosenbergs other than that of the Greenglasses. The Court of Appeals later declared that the case must stand or fall on the testimony of the Greenglasses.

Perhaps the most telling testimony against the two were the words of Elizabeth Bentley, professional informer and anti-Communist writer and lecturer, who said she did not even know and had never seen Julius and Ethel Rosenberg. But she said, and this was really the refrain, the motif of the whole trial, that all Communists were and had to be Soviet spies if such action were asked of them. In the effort to prove the Rosenbergs Communists, the can they had used to collect contributions for Spanish refugee children was a major government exhibit. So was a petition Ethel Rosenberg had signed, along with tens of thousands of others, in the successful election campaign of the late Peter Cacchione, Communist candidate for the New York City Council.

Irving H. Saypol, the federal district attorney who was later rewarded for the Rosenberg convictions by elevation to the New York Supreme Court at a salary of $28,000 a year, declared in his opening statement that the evidence would show fanatical devotion to Communism on the part of Julius Rosenberg, whose "primary loyalty," he said, was therefore to the Soviet Union.

The presiding judge, Irving R. Kaufman, he who said he had received the guidance of God before sentencing the young parents to death in the electric chair, was clearly impressed by the testimony of such witnesses as Bentley. Despite the legal dictum concerning "presumption of innocence," and before the defense had introduced a syllable of evidence, he expressed his conviction that the government had established a case of "tremendous strength."

Judge Kaufman even seemed impressed by a primitive diagram which Greenglass said was a replica of one he had drawn of the atom bomb, and sold to the Russians. It was based on bits of conversation he had overheard at Los Alamos while he worked as a mechanic. Although he had never passed a course in physics and his education had stopped with high school, he said he had detailed the secret of the atom bomb in twelve handwritten pages. The government had announced it would call Dr. Harold C. Urey, leading physicist who had played a prominent part in achieving the bomb. It did not. If it had, Dr. Urey could have demolished Greenglass' testimony by repeating his own testimony before a Congressional committee on March 3, 1946. He had said: "Detailed data on the atomic bomb would require 80 to 90 volumes of close print. Any spies capable of picking up this information would get information more rapidly by staying at home and working in their own laboratories." Even *Time* and *Life* agreed that Greenglass' testimony made little scientific sense and the *Scientific American* expressed doubt that any atomic secret had been really disclosed at the trial.

Because of the political climate, and the latitude offered in the conspiracy charge, the conviction of the Rosenbergs was a foregone conclusion. That the members of any jury which failed to do so would themselves have suffered penalties of one kind or another, in view of the prevailing hysteria, cannot be seriously denied. Due process in this case, and others like it, is only a fiction.

This is essentially the conclusion of one of the foremost legal authorities of our time after a conscientious and prolonged examination of the entire trial record. Few attorneys, either in the United States or Great Britain, are known so widely and favorably for their ability to make a profound, impartial analysis, as is D. N. Pritt, Queen's Counsel, former member of Parliament, former chairman of the Howard League for Penal Reform and the Bentham Committee for Poor Litigants. He was also chairman of the International Committee for Investigation of the Reichstag Fire. His report on the Rosenberg case follows in part:

"Public opinion in more Continents than one has been deeply disturbed by the case of Julius and Ethel Rosenberg, who have now been lying under sentence of death for nearly eighteen months, after a conviction in the United States District Court for the Southern district of New York on a charge of conspiracy, the essence of the charge being that they conspired to obtain by espionage information about the atom bomb and other U. S. military secrets for the benefit of the U. S. S. R., a country which was not of course in a state of war against the U. S. A. during any part of the period covered by the charge, June, 1944 to June, 1950, and was indeed fighting on the same side as the U. S. A. during the most important part of the period.

"I have practiced as an English barrister for 43 years, during which time I have had considerable experience both in trial and in Appellate work. In the latter, I have had to study in detail many hundreds of Records of cases from all parts of the British Empire and Commonwealth, including India, in all of which countries the procedure is very similar to that of the U. S. A.; and I have studied also a certain number of Records from the U. S. A. itself. To read the Record in the Rosenberg case, and to form an estimate of the value which the evidence given in the case should possess in the eyes of impartial lawyers trained in Anglo-Saxon legal traditions and procedure, is thus work of the sort to which I have devoted a large part of my time during my practice as a barrister, particularly during the last twenty years.

"The indictment on which Julius and Ethel Rosenberg were tried was returned on the 31st January, 1951, against five defendants in all—the two Rosenbergs, one Morton Sobell, one Yakovlev, and one David Greenglass. David Greenglass pleaded guilty. The two Rosenbergs and Sobell pleaded not guilty and were tried together, the case of Yakovlev being severed.

"The charge was that the five defendants named, together with one Harry Gold, one Ruth Greenglass, 'and other persons unknown,' had conspired over a period of six years, from the 6th

June, 1944 to the 16th June. 1950, 'the U.S.A. being there and then at war, with intent and reason to believe that it would be used to the advantage of a foreign nation, to wit the U.S.S.R., to communicate, deliver and transmit to a foreign government, to wit the U.S.S.R., and representatives and agents thereof, directly and indirectly, documents, writings, sketches, notes and information relating to the National Defense of the U.S.A.

Conspiracy—A Catch-All

"It is as well to explain at the outset what is the essence of the crime of conspiracy, and why a charge of conspracy to commit some crime or other is so frequently made, in lieu of a charge that the crime was actually committed. 'Conspiracy' can be defined, sufficiently for present purposes, as an agreement between two or more people to commit a crime; it is itself a crime, and the crime of conspiracy is complete as soon as two or more persons have agreed in any way whatsoever, whether formally or informally, by words or by conduct, to commit some crime; it is not necessary for the prosecution to prove the commission of the ultimate crime nor even of facts amounting to an attempt to commit it. It is thus in general easier to secure a conviction for conspiracy than for any other offense, for less has actually to be proved against the defendants; and prejudice or excitement may lead a jury to convict parties on a mere allegation that they agreed or arranged together to do something. under circumstances where, if it were necessary to prove some positive criminal act, the jury would have to acquit because there would be no evidence at all of any such acts. To secure a conviction is moreover made easier still by the operation of a peculiar rule of evidence. In all normal cases no evidence can be given against any defendant in a criminal case except evidence of acts which he himself did or words which he himself spoke; but in a conspiracy case, so long as some evidence—however tenuous—is given from which an agreement between the alleged conspirators might be inferred, the acts and words of any of them, asserted to be done or spoken in pursuance of the conspiracy, are admissible evidence against all the others, on the footing that they are all agents of one another, and so responsible for each other's words and actions.

"The trial took place before Judge Irving R. Kaufman on fourteen days in March, 1951. The prosecution put in a list of 112 witnesses, but in fact called only twenty-two of them, and one other.

"The strength and weakness of the case depends, of course, on these witnesses, on their characters, on what they said, who they were, and what motives or interest they had; and it is thus of the greatest importance to know clearly all these points and to see exactly

"(1) what sort of a reliable case all the witnesses between them were able to build up to establish that the Rosenbergs were guilty at all, and

"(2) how serious anything was that the Rosenbergs were alleged to have done—and, above all. of course, whether what they had done merited the death penalty.

The Unreliability of Greenglass

"The principal witness against the Rosenbergs was David Greenglass. There were an unusually large number of reasons for mistrusting his evidence. To begin with, he had pleaded guilty to the conspiracy for which the Rosenbergs were being tried. but had not yet been brought up for sentence; thus, he might hope, and he expressly said that he did hope, to obtain some advantage for himself as a result of giving evidence against the Rosenbergs; for the Court might ultimately give him a light sentence, and even if it gave him a substantial one, the Government might well remit much or all of it He thus had a strong motive to 'pile it on.' In addition, he was, of course, fully established by his plea of guilty, by his evidence, and by surrounding circumstances (such as his possession of substantial sums of money which could only be explained on the basis that he was telling the truth when he said that he was selling military secrets for money), to have been a party to a conspiracy which both he himself and the prosecution described as a most serious one

"He thus fell into the class of 'accomplice' witnesses, those who, in the old English phrase, 'turn Queen's evidence.' Such witnesses are universally regarded as highly unreliable, not merely because they are self-confessed criminals, and are betraying their associates, but far more because it is dangerously easy for them to implicate falsely, for some benefit to themselves, or to pay off some 'score,' or for other reason, one who in fact took no part in the crime. They are in a position to tell a story that is in the main true, and thus much easier to tell without being exposed as a liar in cross-examination, but at the same time to insert into that story one limited but serious falsity, namely, the assertion that some accused person took part in it when in fact he had nothing to do with it; and, if anything could make this easier, it would be that the accused was related to the accomplice, so that it would be natural for them to meet from time to time.

"If the Government wanted help it should give help. It should give Greenglass 'a pat on the back'; he should be praised, not punished, said his Counsel. Greenglass was, however, given a sentence of fifteen years' imprisonment and his only chance of not serving this fully lies in the hope of leniency from a grateful government.

"(It was also clear, if not perhaps very important, that there had been long disagreements between him and Julius Rosenberg over a business in which they were partners after his demobilization from the army, which eventuated in his instructing his lawyer to bring civil proceedings against Julius.)

David Greenglass' Story

"Nor was that quite all; for Ruth Greenglass, named in the indictment as party to the conspiracy, for some unstated reason not actually indicted, but standing in peril of being indicted at some subsequent time, was David's wife, and he professed to love her dearly. Nevertheless, in the course of the many interviews he had with the F.B.I. (Federal Bureau of Investigation), in which he told bit by bit, as he remembered it, the whole of his story, he betrayed in the very first interview the full tale of his wife's participation in the conspiracy in which he himself, at any rate, was taking part. With such an equipment, David Greenglass might be regarded as a man on whose evidence it would not be safe to convict anyone, but his evidence must of course be examined.

"His version of how he came to take part in the conspiracy was that his wife went down from New York to the neighborhood of Los Alamos, where he was working as a machinist, to take him a message—as she alleged—from Julius Rosenberg, inviting him to take part in espionage, and that by the morning of the following day he had decided to do so! And, at a later stage, when according to him Julius Rosenberg warned him that he was in danger of arrest and ought to leave the country, he accepted from Rosenberg sums amounting to $5,000 in cash to enable him to do so; he stated on oath that he never had any intention of leaving, and that he concealed this intention from Rosenberg but nevertheless accepted and retained the money. He had, he added, such a distaste for the money that he wanted to flush it down the lavatory, but changed his mind and used it to hire Mr. O. John Rogge as his lawyer instead.

"The nature of his evidence against the Rosenbergs lent itself to no sort or kind of corroboration. It contained accounts of conversation with them, at which no third party was present, and of occasions on which he said that he furnished to the Rosenbergs sketches and written descriptions of processes and material objects such as lenses. None of the alleged sketches or descriptions was produced, but Greenglass prepared—four or five years after the alleged incidents, from his own unaided memory—what he said were reproductions of the material, and these were put before the jury. Whether his limited education made it possible for him to do anything of this sort accurately is a matter for scientists rather than lawyers; but from the point of view of a lawyer it can be said that such reproductions, from even the most reliable of witnesses, would add little or nothing to their evidence and could not in any way constitute corroboration.

Death Sentence Unwarranted

"That not merely a conviction but a sentence of death should be based upon such evidence runs counter, in my opinion, to all normal standards of criminal procedure and of the administration of justice.

"I should add that, even if the evidence were regarded as providing a reliable basis for conviction, there would still be lacking, in my humble opinion, any good reason for imposing or upholding a death sentence. Such a sentence could surely only be justified if it were clear that the secret information involved was of the utmost importance.

"While scientists can plainly make more effective comment than I can on this part of the evidence, I can assert as a lawyer that there was nothing in it to show that the information which David Greenglass claimed to have communicated to Julius Rosenberg was of any especial value or danger, such as to justify on any view the death penalty.

"David Greenglass's wife, Ruth, whose position has already been explained, also gave evidence, which followed pretty closely that of her husband, and is equally devoid of any corroboration. It does not call for separate study; her hopes and fears for herself and her husband, her readiness to confess to crime and to implicate relatives in that crime, do not differ from her husband's. In

37

a sense she can be said to corroborate her husband, but this could not be regarded as independent corroboration.

"The evidence of the two Greenglasses was almost the only evidence against the Rosenbergs; but it is necessary just to examine what other evidence there was. I begin with Max Elitcher, a man who had worked in the Bureau of Ordnance of the Navy Department. He was mainly a witness against the other defendant, Sobell, but he did say that on three occasions Julius Rosenberg asked him to obtain confidential information for him, for Soviet purposes. He said, however, that he had not done so; he said, moreover, in cross-examination, that two of his three meetings with Rosenberg were merely social.

"Elitcher made it quite plain that he himself was an accomplice. As he said, 'I was part of it.' He admitted, too, that ne had told lies under oath, and that, being 'scared to death,' he had told the F.B.I. 'everything he knew'—although he had lied to them too—in the hope that he might 'come out the best way' and that 'nothing would happen to him.' For some unexplained reason, he was neither indicted nor even mentioned in the indictment as a co-conspirator.

Verdict Based on Hysteria

"Of the remaining seventeen prosecution witnesses, only four gave evidence of anything the Rosenbergs were alleged to have said or done. Dorothy Abel, the sister of Ruth Greenglass, gave evidence that she had once been asked to leave the room whilst her sister talked with Julius Rosenberg and that the latter had once in her presence praised the Soviet system and described the U.S.A. as 'capitalistic'! A Dr. Bernhardt, Julius Rosenberg's physician, proved that Rosenberg asked him in 1950 what inoculations were needed for anyone entering Mexico. Two other witnesses, a Mrs. Cox and a Mr. Schneider, gave evidence 'in rebuttal,' after the close of the defendants' case, about the Rosenbergs on points that may fairly be left unmentioned as trivial. The remaining thirteen witnesses either gave no evidence at all that bore on the Rosenbergs, or merely mentioned their names as hearsay.

"Thus, the prosecution case against the Rosenbergs rested on the evidence of three persons, two of them husband and wife, and all of them unreliable as accomplices and for other reasons too. I am unable to believe that, if the case had not involved political topics or had not been heard at a period when hysteria and prejudice played so strong a role, evidence so weak would have been put forward by the prosecution in any country in the world which followed the Anglo-Saxon traditions and procedure. I think that under those conditions any Court would almost certainly have withdrawn the case from the jury. But this case was allowed to go to the jury and the Rosenbergs were not only convicted but were sentenced to death.

"The Rosenbergs, who at every stage asserted their innocence, gave evidence and called two other witnesses; these latter dealt with points which can fairly be regarded as unimportant. In a study designed to examine the strength or weakness of the prosecution case which the jury accepted, what the Rosenbergs themselves said is not of quite such importance as what the prosecution did or did not prove; but it remains true that they did give evidence, being of course submitted to cross-examination and answering fully and consistently everything that was alleged against them. Nothing was established against their character, unless it be that they had talked of the Soviet economic system, had thought that the Soviet Union was at one stage bearing the brunt of the Second World War, and had had in their possession a collecting box for Spanish refugee children.

"I must say a little about the conduct of the trial. The prosecution, both in the opening statement of the prosecuting attorney and throughout the evidence, repeatedly made play with the alleged Communist connections of the Rosenbergs; the usual 'warning' was given that of course communism is not evidence of conspiracy or of espionage, and was immediately nullified by the assertion—wholly unproved—that Communists are more likely to commit espionage than other people.

"But these remarks by the judge are, alas, not the worst part of the matter. He went on to treat the case as if the information which the Rosenbergs were said to have communicated to the U.S.S.R.—of the value of which, as I have already mentioned, there was no real evidence—had been established to be of the most fundamental importance. He began, for example, with the assertion that what the Rosenbergs had done 'has already caused, in my opinion, the Communist aggression in Korea' (about which, of course, there was once again no evidence). He went even further and based his determination on sentence on the wholly unproved assumption that the Rosenbergs had obtained from David Greenglass and given to the U.S.S.R. just the vital information that enabled that country to develop the atom bomb, which it could not have achieved without that information. The Rosenbergs had thus, as he put it, 'altered the history of the world' to

39

the injury of the U.S.A. (Incidentally, although it could have been alleged in the indictment that the conspirators had acted with intent to injure the U.S.A., no such allegation was pleaded.)

Judicial Bias

"I am forced to the conclusion that, even if the conviction of the Rosenbergs had rested on reliable evidence that they had conspired to obtain some information, any sentence expressed by the judge to be based on such inaccurate and unproved assertions as to the importance of the information would have to be set aside on appeal under any procedure which provided for a free review of the sentence by an Appellate Court. Unfortunately the procedure applicable to this case does not provide for such a review, any more than it provides for a consideration of the credibility of the witnesses or the reliability of the evidence. Were the procedure different, it may well be that the whole matter would have been disposed of already. But there is, in effect, no appeal at all to any court from either of the main defects of this trial, namely, the unreliability of the evidence and the gravely excessive sentence. The duty of securing a review on these points thus rests on public opinion throughout the world. After full study, for the reasons which I have expressed above, I must express the view, from a purely professional standpoint, that it would offend against all Anglo-Saxon standards of justice that the convictions, let alone the sentences, of the Rosenbergs should be allowed to stand."

V. "MR. PRESIDENT—SAVE THESE LIVES!"

THESE ARE THE FACTS, then, that have resulted in appeals to President Truman for clemency from every part of the United States, from every quarter of the globe, from people of every shade of opinion, of every color, creed, and political belief. There are those who have asked President Truman to commute the death sentences not on the basis of the evidence but on the basis of their unprecedented savagery, not on the basis of the Rosenbergs' alleged guilt or innocence, but on the grounds that there is no justice or equity in death sentences against the two young parents when virtually every other person charged with a similar crime has received a sentence of only a comparatively few years imprisonment.

Not only do such letters and wires to President Truman point to the ten years sentence of Axis Sally and Tokyo Rose for wartime treason, and a series of similar crimes and sentences; but they also emphasize to President Truman that he even granted mercy and commutation of the death sentence to the misguided Collazo who killed a Blair House guard in his admitted attempt to assassinate the President. They point, too, to the fact that late in November, 1952, an air force sergeant in Korea was arrested for selling secrets of our latest jet planes even as soldiers were dying in Korea —and that under the army court martial the severest punishment he faced was not death but life imprisonment.

But the Rosenbergs, arrested and tried in time of peace, charged with giving secrets not to a foe, but to a war-time

41

ally, are sentenced to death. Those who ask clemency on this basis, believe the Rosenbergs innocent but they add: "Even if the prosecution's case were true, it would be the case of two young misguided idealists trying to win the war against the Nazis by aiding the strongest ally of the United States in what was then a war for survival." The indictment does not even charge, as most such indictments do, a crime that worked against the welfare of the United States.

It is because of such radical inequities in this case, as compared with other similar cases, that the charge of anti-Semitism will not down. For that matter the charge does not have to be argued. Fascist organizations are flooding the country, or at least some sections of it, with stickers bearing the slogan "The Rosenbergs Must Die!" The authorities report that they have an unprecedented number of requests to witness the scheduled execution on the part of those who say they desire the pleasure of seeing the Rosenbergs die. The Pentagon Patriots, of Washington D. C., have sent widely through the mails a poem called "The Rosenbergs Must Die," the last verse of which reads:

> *"These Rosenbergs*
> *Must burn and die*
> *If they cheat death*
> *The Stars and Stripes*
> *May cease to fly!"*

Because of such phenomena, and others, there is the smell of Buchenwald about this case. Once they charged Jews, as in the Mendel Bailis case in Czarist Russia, with blood rituals, and used the charge for pogroms, but in the present they use the more streamlined tactic of charging crimes connected with the dread and mysterious atom bomb. Jews recall, too, in thinking of the aspect of a brother sending his sister to death, the famous case in Austria-Hungary in 1881 when a boy testified that he saw his own father

42

and mother drinking Christian blood in a Jewish ritual. He confessed later that he had been forced so to testify in fear that he himself would be killed if he did not. But David Greenglass cannot confess, even though he could not be tried under the double jeopardy rule, without risking the arrest and trial of his wife on a charge bearing the death penalty.

It is widely remembered now that Irving Saypol, the Jewish federal attorney who prosecuted the Rosenbergs, was admonished by the Court of Appeals in August, 1951 for his appeals to "racial prejudice" against a Jewish witness in the Remington case. And it is recalled, too, that Judge Kaufman, before sentencing to death those he could well have sentenced to a prison term, dwelt long on his prayers in the synagogue.

It is for these reasons, including Saypol's "reward" of a $28,000 a year judgeship, that many Jewish leaders and newspapers have found the taint of anti-Semitism in this cruel case. The *Jewish Daily Forward,* on April 6, 1951; the *Jewish Day,* on April 8, expressed grave doubts about the sentence and expressed the hope, in the words of the *Day,* "that a way will be found to set aside the death sentence." And Rabbi Louis D. Gross, publisher of the *Jewish Examiner,* asked on March 14, 1952: "Why did Judge Kaufman impose the extreme penalty? Did he think the sentences were necessary to counteract the anti-Semitic charge of Communism against Jews in general? Apparently this jurist had not learned that anti-Semitism has nothing to do with the truth." With a third of the population of New York Jewish, there was not one Jewish member of the jury.

The trade unions and their members are active in protesting the Rosenberg case, labor's memory going back to the Haymarket case of 1886 in Chicago when leaders of the eight-hour-day movement were framed and executed for murders they did not commit. Judge Gary, who heard the case and imposed the sentences that Governor Altgeld afterwards formally found were obtained through a rigged jury and perjured testimony, was promoted to the chairmanship of the United States Steel Corporation. He had his job and the defendants were dead when it was found that it was a tragic "mistake" —that the men were innocent.

Labor is determined that innocence shall not be established after the Rosenbergs die, that they shall be granted life and the chance to prove their innocence now. Its members well recall that Tom Mooney was framed and found guilty on an airtight case, the perfect case, or so it seemed, of throwing a bomb; and that Mooney was sentenced to death and that for a time there was scarcely a person who did not believe him guilty. But the labor movement organized and fought and proved him innocent and saved his life. Not the least of the Rosenbergs' crimes, it should always be remembered, was that they were staunch and militant trade union members always on the firing line.

Trade union members have been trained in the niceties of frame-up through so often being its victims. They know that a frame-up is most often a part of policy aimed at the living standards of the working class. They know there is a connection between the Taft-Hartley anti-Communist indictments against members of the labor movement and the Rosenberg case. They know that both are a part of the drive to war, both an effort to behead the peace movement, both directed at all protests against high prices, high profits, and low real wages. They can see a general offensive gathering force against the trade union movement and an increasing number are realizing that such cases as that of the Rosenbergs are part of this offensive.

If, however, there are any who doubt it, they should ask Harold Ward, Negro trade union leader at the Harvester Company in Chicago, who was recently framed and charged with murder as he led a strike against that company. He knows that success in frame-up against the Rosenbergs emboldens and encourages those reactionary forces which have framed him and are eager to frame others. He feels that if the fight to save the Rosenbergs had already been successful it would have been exceedingly doubtful if he himself would now be facing the electric chair. Frame-up grows. Frame-up spreads. And it is always used for policy, to accomplish specific aims of reaction.

But the Negro people, the great Negro people, see through this atomic frame-up with clearer eye than any other Americans. For generations they have been framed for a crime, consciously selected as one so horrible that it would serve the political purpose of separating them and alienating them from white Americans—the charge of "rape." They understand the special nature of the crime, the frame-up, so often charged against them and they understand the special nature of the crime being charged against radicals to separate them from the American people —treason, espionage, giving the secret of our new savior, the atom bomb, to a foreign power.

"Tell them why I died," said the martyred Willie McGee as they strapped him into Mississippi's portable electric chair in 1951. "Tell them to fight on." He was speaking of his children, fatherless now through frame-up. Can Americans afford to let these things continue much longer?

Julius Rosenberg does not think so. Writing of Willie McGee's execution, Rosenberg, himself in the death house and writing to his wife, also there, said:

> "Ethel, I was terribly shocked to read that Willie McGee was executed. My heart is sad, my eyes are filled with tears. My heart hurts at crimes which have been directed so long against the Negro people. Shame on those who perpetrated this heinous act! Greater shame on those who did not protest! It seems to me that the federal courts are using tactics so long applied to Negroes, legal lynching,

45

and are now attempting, as in our case, to extend
the lynching to political prisoners."

All of the shibboleths and slogans that white Americans
use to conceal and decorate injustice do not really conceal it
from the Negro people. Their eyes are clear. For that reason
some of their greatest leaders have spoken out on the Rosenberg case: Paul Robeson, known, loved, and respected the
world over for his fight for peace; W. E. B. DuBois, histori-
an, anthropologist, poet; William L. Patterson, who writes
an introduction to this pamphlet as head of the Civil Rights
Congress, and who has traveled from coast to coast address-
ing great crowds on the Rosenberg case.

The venerable Dr. DuBois, himself framed (but later
acquitted) on a charge of advocating peace, said of the
Rosenbergs:

"The significance of the Rosenberg case reaches beyond
the fate of two individuals, tragic as that may be. It becomes a part of the great peace crusade. In the midst of
war and fear of war we do unbelievable things, we rush to
lying, slander and hate because we fear what war will do to
us and to ours. In blind recoil from mass murder we do anything which in our fevered imagination seems likely to save
us from war. This is the reason why here in a nation born in
peace and justice, we are almost without protest committing
crimes against humanity, against elementary civil rights,
against every ideal of democracy.

"The public opinion which crucifies a father and mother
in the prime of life is based on the abject fear of disaster to
the whole nation. But fear is not fact, and ignorantly to
commit an unforgiveable crime in the name of a greater
crime is no excuse."

If not in the name of justice, then in the name of the
national welfare—although the two forever go together—
the Rosenbergs must not die. In far-off Africa, on the high

mountains of Tibet, on the streets of Paris and near Trafalgar Square, men and women still speak of how we murdered Sacco, killed Vanzetti, and the fact that we admit their innocence now is to no avail. They are dead, slain by a bureaucracy disdainful of their lives and innocence. Injustice such as this becomes a legend and grows from tongue to tongue and never dies; and years later, it is part of what men are thinking when they write on walls: "Americans, Go Home."

The Rosenbergs must not die, if Americans are to save themselves. As Ethel Rosenberg wrote as she sat in the cell of Sing Sing's death house, Americans must "rally in ever increasing numbers to the Rosenberg defense and their own. For they who have the courage and the foresight and the decency to aid the Rosenbergs' fight for freedom ensure their own eventual release."

CRC Publications

WE CHARGE GENOCIDE   cloth $2.50; paper $1

The historic petition to the United Nations, edited by William L. Patterson, charging the U.S. Government with violations of the UN Convention on Prevention and Punishment of Genocide, through systematic persecution and killing of the Negro people.

THE REIGN OF WITCHES, by Elizabeth Lawson
35 cents

The dramatic story of the successful mass struggle against the Alien and Sedition Acts of 1798.

RED TAPE & BARBED WIRE, by Sender Garlin
25 cents

The plans for American concentration camps.

(Tear off and mail)

□□□

CIVIL RIGHTS CONGRESS
23 West 26th Street
New York 10, N. Y.

☐ I enclose $........ Please send me ...... copies of the pamphlet "The Cold-War Murder." (Bundles of 10 or more copies, 15 cents each; bundles of 200 or more copies, 12½ cents each).

☐ I want to join the Civil Rights Congress. Here is $1 for my 1953 membership.

Name ....

Address ....

City............................ Zone...... State...........